WATERFORD CARDIGAN

BEGINNER

SIZES
S (M, L, 1X, 2X)

Finished Bust 38 (42, 46, 50, 54) in.
(96.5 (106.5, 117, 127, 137) cm)

Finished Length 32 (33, 33, 33 34) in.
(81.5 (84, 84, 84, 86.5) cm)

Note: Pattern is written for smallest size with changes for larger sizes in parentheses. When only one number is given, it applies to all sizes. To follow pattern more easily, circle all numbers pertaining to your size before beginning.

MATERIALS
LION BRAND® WOOL-EASE® THICK & QUICK®
#124 Barley 7 (8, 9, 9, 10) balls
or color of your choice
LION BRAND knitting needles size 13 (9 mm)
LION BRAND stitch holder
LION BRAND large-eyed blunt needle

ADDITIONAL MATERIALS
4 buttons, 1 in. (25 mm) diameter

Satchel Grande

PATTERN STITCH
Seed Stitch (odd number of sts)
Row 1 (RS): *K1, p1; rep from * to last st, k1.

Row 2: P the knits and k the purls.
Rep Row 2 for Seed st.

BAG
Cast on 35 sts. Beginning with a p row, work in St st (k on RS, p on WS) for 9 rows (for casing). Increase 12 sts evenly across next row – 47 sts. Place markers on each side edge. Work in Seed st for 11 in. (28 cm). Place markers on each side edge. Work in Seed st for 6 in. (15 cm) more. Place markers on each side edge. Continue in Seed st for 11 in. (28 cm), end with a WS row. Place markers on each side edge. K 1 row, decreasing 12 sts evenly across row. Continue in St st, beginning with a p row, for 9 rows (for casing). Bind off.

SIDE PANELS (make 2)
Cast on 15 sts. Work in Seed st for 11 in. (28 cm). Bind off.

FINISHING
Sew Side Panels to sides of Bag, aligning corners and lower edges of Side Panels with markers. Fold St st casing in half to inside of Bag and sew in place. Slide dowels into casings and sew ends closed.

HANDLES (make 2)
Cast on 5 sts. Work in Seed st for 25 in. (63.5 cm). Bind off. Sew long side edges together. Sew each end of Handle securely to inside edge of casing, about 3 in. (7.5 cm) from end of dowel.

EARTH BLOCK AFGHAN

Shown on page 7.

 **EASY**

SIZE
42 x 56 in. (106.5 x 142 cm)

MATERIALS
LION BRAND® WOOL-EASE® THICK & QUICK®
 #123 Oatmeal 4 balls (A)
 #149 Charcoal 4 balls (B)
 #124 Barley 4 balls (C)
 or colors of your choice
LION BRAND crochet hook size P-15 (10 mm)
LION BRAND large-eyed blunt needle

GAUGE
One Block = 14 in. (35.5 cm) square.
BE SURE TO CHECK YOUR GAUGE.

BLOCK (make 12 – 4 each with A, B and C)
Chain 24.

> **TIP**
> While thick yarn is ideal for accessories, it also makes terrific sweaters and jackets. For beginners and for quick projects, the combination of a super chunky yarn with larger needles is a winner.

Row 1: Half double crochet in third chain from hook and in each chain across – 22 half double crochet.

Rows 2–16: Chain 2, turn. Half double crochet in each stitch across.
Fasten off.

FINISHING

Following Assembly Diagram, sew Blocks together.
Weave in ends.

A	C	B
B	A	C
C	B	A
A	C	B

(A) #123 Oatmeal
(B) #149 Charcoal
(C) #124 Barley

Wool-Ease® Thick & Quick® is the super bulky member of the Wool-Ease family. It has the feel, warmth, and softness of wool with the easy care of acrylic. Perfect for extra warm items, Wool-Ease Thick & Quick works up quickly, easily, and is an ideal yarn for beginners as well as advanced yarn crafters.

About Lion Brand® Yarn Company

Lion Brand Yarn Company is America's oldest hand knitting yarn brand. Founded in 1878, Lion Brand Yarn Company is a leading supplier of quality hand knitting and crochet yarns. Throughout its history, Lion Brand Yarn has been at the forefront of yarn trends while consistently providing its customers with the highest quality product at a value price. The company's mission is to provide ideas, inspiration and education to yarn crafters.

SATCHEL GRANDE

EASY

SIZE

11 in. high x 18 in. wide x 6 in. deep (28 x 45.5 x 15 cm)

MATERIALS

LION BRAND® WOOL-EASE® THICK & QUICK®
    #149 Charcoal 4 balls
    or color of your choice
LION BRAND knitting needles size 11 (8 mm)
LION BRAND split ring markers
LION BRAND large-eyed blunt needle

ADDITIONAL MATERIALS

2 wood dowels ½ in. (13 mm) diameter x 15 in (38 cm) long

GAUGE

10½ sts = 4 in. (10 cm) in Seed stitch.
BE SURE TO CHECK YOUR GAUGE.

TIP Need markers and don't have any? Take some cotton in a bright color (Lion® Cotton is ideal) and make as many little loops as you need. Cotton markers are great because they won't slip.

GAUGE

8 stitches and 12 rows = 4 in. (10 cm) in Stockinette stitch
(knit on right side, purl on wrong side).
BE SURE TO CHECK YOUR GAUGE.

NOTE

Cardigan is worked in one piece beginning at lower back.

CARDIGAN

Cast on 38 (42, 46, 50, 54) stitches. Work in Garter stitch
(knit every row) for 8 rows for edging. Change to Stockinette
stitch (knit on right side, purl on wrong side) and work until
piece measures 24 in. (61 cm) from beginning, end with a
wrong side row.

Shape Sleeves
Next Row (right side): Knit 38 (42, 46, 50, 54), cast on
18 stitches – 56 (60, 64, 68, 72) stitches.

Next Row: Purl 56 (60, 64, 68, 72), cast on 18 stitches –
74 (78, 82, 86, 90) stitches.
Continue in Stockinette stitch until Sleeve measures 6 (7, 7,
7, 8) in. (15 (18, 18, 18, 20.5) cm), end with a right side row.

Shape Neck
Next Row (wrong side): Purl 26 (28, 30, 32, 34),
knit 22 for neck edging, purl 26 (28, 30, 32, 34).

Next Row: Knit.
Repeat last 2 rows 3 times.

Divide for Fronts
Next Row (wrong side): Purl 26 (28, 30, 32, 34), knit 5, slip these 31 (33, 35, 37, 39) stitches to a stitch holder for Left Front, bind off 12 stitches for back neck; knit 5, purl 26 (28, 30, 32, 34).
Continue on 31 (33, 35, 37, 39) stitches just worked for Right Front.

Right Front
Next Row (right side): Knit 31 (33, 35, 37, 39).

Next Row: Knit 5, purl 26 (28, 30, 32, 34).
Repeat last 2 rows for 3 in. (7.5 cm), end with a wrong side row.

Shape Neck
Row 1 (right side): Knit 31 (33, 35, 37, 39), cast on 17 stitches – 48 (50, 52, 54, 56) stitches.

Row 2: Knit 22, purl to end of row.

Row 3: Knit.

Row 4: Knit 2, bind off 2 stitches for buttonhole, knit 14, bind off 2 stitches for 2nd buttonhole, knit 2, purl to end of row.

Row 5: Knit, cast on 2 stitches over each set of bound-off stitches of previous row.

Rows 6 and 8: Repeat Row 2.

Rows 7 and 9: Knit.

NOTE: Before continuing on the Right Front, read the section below that begins with ***.

Row 10: Knit 5, purl to end of row.

Rows 11–18: Repeat Rows 9 and 10.

Row 19: Knit to last 4 stitches, bind off 2 stitches (buttonhole), knit 2.

Row 20: Knit 2, cast on 2 stitches, knit 1, purl to end of row.

Rows 21–30: Repeat Rows 9 and 10.

Rows 31 and 32: Repeat Rows 19 and 20.

***AND AT THE SAME TIME, when Sleeve measures 16 (18, 18, 18, 20) in. (40.5 (46, 46, 46, 51) cm), end with a wrong side row.

Shape Body
Next Row (right side): Bind off 18 stitches for Sleeve, knit to end of row.
Continue to work in Stockinette st, keeping 5 stitches at front edge in Garter stitch, until piece measures 22 in. (56 cm) from Sleeve bind-off row.
Knit 8 rows for Garter edging. Bind off.

Left Front
Slip stitches from stitch holder back onto needle and join yarn.

Next Row (right side): Knit.

Next Row: Purl 26 (28, 30, 32, 34), knit 5.
Repeat last 2 rows for 3 in. (7.5 cm), end with a right side row.

Shape Neck
Row 1 (wrong side): Purl 26 (28, 30, 32, 34), knit 5, cast on 17 stitches – 48 (50, 52, 54, 56) stitches.

Row 2: Knit.

Row 3: Purl 26 (28, 30, 32, 34), knit to end of row.
Repeat Rows 2 and 3 three times.

Next Row (right side): Knit.

Next Row: Purl to last 5 stitches, knit 5.
Repeat last 2 rows until Sleeve measures 16 (18, 18, 18, 20) in. (40.5 (46, 46, 46, 51) cm), end with a right side row.

Shape Body
Next Row: Bind off 18 stitches, purl to last 5 stitches, knit 5.
Continue to work in Stockinette stitch, keeping 5 stitches at front edge in Garter stitch, until piece measures same as Right Front to Garter edging. Knit 8 rows. Bind off.

FINISHING
Sleeve Edging
From right side, pick up and knit about 32 (36, 36, 36, 40) stitches evenly spaced along wrist edge of Sleeve. Knit 8 rows. Bind off. Repeat on other Sleeve.
Sew side and Sleeve seams. Sew on buttons opposite buttonholes.
Weave in ends.

FLOPPY BERET

 **EASY**

SIZE
One Size

Finished Circumference 22½ in. (57.5 cm)

MATERIALS
LION BRAND® WOOL-EASE® THICK & QUICK®
     #110 Navy 2 balls
     or color of your choice
LION BRAND crochet hook size N-13 (9 mm)
LION BRAND stitch marker
LION BRAND large-eyed blunt needle

GAUGE
7 sc = 4 in. (10 cm).
BE SURE TO CHECK YOUR GAUGE.

STITCH EXPLANATION
sc2tog (sc dec) Insert hook into st and draw up a loop.
Insert hook into next st and draw up a loop. Yarn over, draw
through all 3 loops on hook.

> **TIP**
> If you have trouble working with a dark colored
> yarn, put a white pillowcase beneath your work,
> it makes the stitches stand out.

BERET

Ch 3; join with sl st in first ch to form a ring.

Rnd 1: Ch 1, work 8 sc in ring; join with sl st in first sc –
8 sc. Place marker for beg of rnd, move marker up as each
rnd is completed.

Rnd 2: Ch 1, 2 sc in each st around; join with sl st in first
sc – 16 sts.

Rnd 3: Ch 1, *sc in next st, 2 sc in next st; rep from
* around; join with sl st in first sc – 24 sts.

Rnd 4: Ch 1, *sc in each of next 2 sts, 2 sc in next st;
rep from * around; join with sl st in first sc – 32 sts.

Rnd 5: Ch 1, *sc in each of next 3 sts, 2 sc in next st;
rep from * around; join with sl st in first sc – 40 sts.

Rnd 6: Ch 1, *sc in each of next 4 sts, 2 sc in next st;
rep from * around; join with sl st in first sc – 48 sts.

Rnd 7: Ch 1, *sc in each of next 5 sts, 2 sc in next st;
rep from * around; join with sl st in first sc – 56 sts.

Rnd 8: Ch 1, *sc in each of next 6 sts, 2 sc in next st; rep from * around; join with sl st in first sc – 64 sts.

Rnds 9–14: Ch 1, turn, sc in each st around; join with sl st in beg ch.

Rnd 15: Ch 1, *sc in each of next 6 sts, sc2tog; rep from * around; join with sl st in first sc – 56 sts.

Rnd 16: Ch 1, *sc in each of next 5 sts, sc2tog; rep from * around; join with sl st in first sc – 48 sts.

Rnd 17: Ch 1, *sc in each of next 4 sts, sc2tog; rep from * around; join with sl st in first sc – 40 sts.

Rnds 18 and 19: Ch 1, turn, working in back loops only, sc in each st around; join with sl st in first sc.
Fasten off.

FINISHING
Weave in ends.

WINTER LACE AFGHAN

Afghan (including borders) is knit in one piece for fast finishing.

 **EASY +**

SIZE
About 46 x 54 in. (117 x 137 cm)

MATERIALS
LION BRAND® WOOL-EASE® THICK & QUICK®
#099 Fisherman 8 balls
or color of your choice
LION BRAND circular knitting needle size 11 (8 mm) 29 in. (73.5 cm) long
LION BRAND large-eyed blunt needle

GAUGE
8 sts + 13 rows = 4 in. (10 cm) in Lace Pattern.
BE SURE TO CHECK YOUR GAUGE.

STITCH EXPLANATIONS
sk2p- slip 1 st as if to knit, knit 2 sts together, pass slipped stitch over – 2 sts decreased.

> **TIP**
> Along with your knitting needles and yarn, it is helpful to have a tape measure, calculator, scissors, stitch holders, stitch markers, point protectors, needle gauge, and crochet hook for picking up stitches, large-eyed blunt needle, and an extra copy of your pattern.

PATTERN STITCHES
Seed St (over odd number of sts)
Row 1: *K1, p1, rep from * across, end k1.

Row 2: Knit the p sts and purl the k sts.
Rep Row 2 for Seed st.

Lace Pattern
Row 1: K1, * yo, ssk, k7, k2tog, yo, k1; rep from * across.

Row 2 and all WS rows: Purl.

Row 3: K1, * k1, yo, ssk, k5, k2tog, yo, k2; rep from * across.

Row 5: K1, * (yo, ssk) twice, k3, (k2tog, yo) twice, k1; rep from * across.

Row 7: K1, * k1, (yo, ssk) twice, k1, (k2tog, yo) twice, k2; rep from * across.

Row 9: K1, * (yo, ssk) twice, yo, sk2p, yo, (k2tog, yo) twice, k1; rep from * across.

Row 11: K1, * k3, k2tog, yo, k1, yo, ssk, k4; rep from * across.

Row 13: K1, * k2, k2tog, yo, k3, yo, ssk, k3; rep from * across.

Row 15: K1, * k1, (k2tog, yo) twice, k1, (yo, ssk) twice, k2; rep from * across.

Row 17: K1, * (k2tog, yo) twice, k3, (yo, ssk) twice, k1; rep from * across.

Row 19: K2tog, yo, * (k2tog, yo) twice, k1, (yo, ssk) twice, yo, sk2p, yo; rep from * across, end (k2tog, yo) twice, k1, (yo, ssk) 3 times.

Row 20: Purl.
Rep Rows 1-20 for Lace Pattern.

AFGHAN
Notes:
1. Circular needle is used to accommodate large number of sts. Work back and forth on circular needle as
if working on straight needles.
2. When working in Lace Pattern, be sure to count your stitches at the end of each row. The stitch count should remain the same at the end of each row.

Cast on 95 sts.
Rows 1-6: Work in Seed st.

Row 7: Work in Seed st as established over first 5 sts, p to last 5 sts, work in Seed st to end of row.

Row 8: Keeping first and last 5 sts in Seed st, work Row 1 of Lace Pattern over center 85 sts.
Continue as established, keeping first and last 5 sts in Seed st and working Lace Pattern over center 85 sts, until 8 reps of Rows 1-20 of Lace Pattern have been completed. Work 6 rows in Seed st. Bind off.

FINISHING Weave in ends.

POCKETED OCTOBER SCARF

 **EASY**

SIZE

10 x 60 in. (25.5 x 152.5 cm)

MATERIALS

LION BRAND® WOOL-EASE® THICK & QUICK®
> #122 Taupe 3 skeins (A)
> #178 Cilantro 3 skeins (B)
> or colors of your choice

LION BRAND knitting needles size 17 (13 mm)
LION BRAND stitch holder
LION BRAND stitch markers
LION BRAND large-eyed blunt needle

GAUGE

8 sts + 12 rows = 4 in. (10 cm) over St st (k on RS, p on WS)
with 1 strand each of A and B held together.
BE SURE TO CHECK YOUR GAUGE.

Pocketed October Scarf | 23

STITCH EXPLANATION

M1 (make 1) An increase worked by lifting the horizontal thread lying between the needles and placing it onto left needle. Knit this new stitch through the back loop.

POCKET LINING (make 1)

With 1 strand each of A and B held together, cast on 12 sts. Work in St st (k on RS, p on WS) for 6 in. (15 cm), end with a WS row. Slip these sts onto stitch holder.

SCARF

With 1 strand each of A and B held together, cast on 20 sts. Knit 6 rows.

Next row (WS): K4, purl to last 4 sts, k4.

Next row (RS): Knit.
Rep last 2 rows until piece measures 8 in. (20 cm) from beg, end with a WS row.
Knit 5 rows.

Next row (WS): K4, bind off 12 sts for pocket, k3. (There will 4 sts on each side of bind off).

Attach Pocket Lining

Next row (RS): K4, with RS facing, k across 12 sts of lining from holder, k4 – 20 sts.

Next row: K4, purl to last 4 sts, k4.

Next row: Knit.
Rep last 2 rows until piece measures 16 in. (40.5 cm), end with a WS row.

Shape Collar

Next row (RS): K4, M1, place marker, k to end of row – 21 sts.

Next row: K4, purl to marker, k to end.

Next row: K to marker, M1, knit to end – 22 sts.
Rep last 2 rows 8 times more – 30 sts. Work even in pattern as established until piece measures 35 in. (89 cm), end with a WS row.

Next row (RS): K to 2 sts before marker, k2tog, k to end – 29 sts.

TIP

Knitting terms on the Internet:

FO	Finished object
UFO	Unfinished object
FROG	Ripping out a project (rip-it, Rip-it)
TINK	To take out a few stitches or rows a.k.a. un-KNIT
SEX	Stash enhancement expedition
KIP	Knit in public

Next row: K4, purl to last 4 sts, k4.
Rep last 2 rows 9 times more – 20 sts. Work even in pattern as established until piece measures 50 in. (127 cm) from beg, end with a WS row.

Next row (RS): K4, slip next 12 sts to a holder, cast on 12 sts, k4 – 20 sts.
Knit 6 rows.

Next row (WS): K4, purl to last 4 sts, k4.

Next row: Knit.
Rep last 2 rows until piece measures 6 in. (15 cm) above sts on holder, end with a WS row.
Knit 6 rows. Bind off.

Second Pocket Lining

With RS facing, slip 12 sts from holder back to needle.
Join yarn and work in St st for 6 in. (15 cm). Bind off.

FINISHING

Sew Pocket Linings in place. Weave in ends.

GENERAL INSTRUCTIONS

ABBREVIATIONS

beg = begin(ning)
ch = chain
cm = centimeters
dec = decreas(e)(s)(ing)
k = knit
k2tog = knit 2 together
M1 = make one
mm = millimeters
p = purl
rep = repeat(s)(ing
rnd(s) = round(s)
RS = right side
sc = single crochet
ssk = slip, slip, knit
sk2p = slip 1 as if to knit, knit 2 together,
psso = pass slipped stitch over
sl st = slip stitch
st(s) = stitch(es)
St st = Stockinette stitch
tog = together
tr = treble (triple) crochet
WS = wrong side
yo = yarn over

* — When you see an asterisk used within a pattern row, the symbol indicates that later you will be told to repeat a portion of the instruction. Most often the instructions will say, repeat from * so many times.

( ) or [ ] — Set off a short number of stitches that are repeated or indicated additional information.

GAUGE

Never underestimate the importance of gauge. Achieving the correct gauge assures that the finished size of your piece matches the finished size given in the pattern.

CHECKING YOUR GAUGE

Work a swatch that is at least 4" (10 cm) square. Use the suggested needle or hook size and the number of stitches given. If your swatch is larger than 4" (10 cm), you need to work it again using a smaller hook; if it is smaller than 4" (10 cm), try it with a larger hook. The same concept applies if you are knitting. If your swatch is larger, work it again with smaller needles. If your swatch is larger, try smaller needles. This might require a swatch or two to get the exact gauge given in the pattern.

METRICS

As a handy reference, keep in mind that 1 ounce = approximately 28 grams and 1" = 2.5 centimeters.

TERMS

continue in this way or as established — Once a pattern is set up (established), the instructions may tell you to continue in the same way.

fasten off — To end your piece, you need to simply pull the yarn through the last loop left on the hook. This keeps the last stitch intact and prevents the work from unraveling.

right side — Refers to the front of the piece.

work even — This is used to indicate an area worked as established without increasing or decreasing.

MARKERS

As a convenience to you, we have used markers to help distinguish the beginning of a pattern. Place markers as instructed. You may use purchased markers or tie a length of contrasting color yarn around the needle. When you reach a marker on each row, slip it from the left needle to the right needle; remove it when no longer needed.

KNIT 2 TOGETHER
   (abbreviated k2tog)
Insert the right needle into the front of the first two stitches on the left needle as if to knit (Fig. 1), then knit them together as if they were one stitch.

Fig. 1

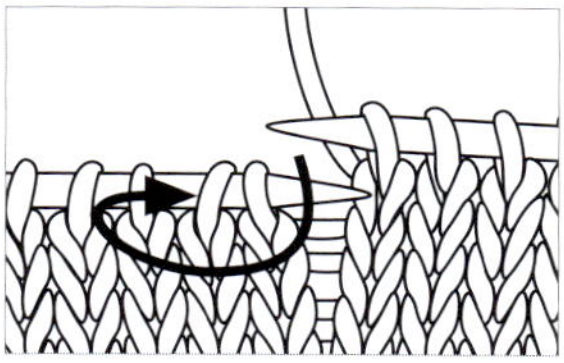

SLIP 1, KNIT 2 TOGETHER, PASS SLIPPED STITCH OVER (abbreviated sk2p)

Slip one stitch as if to knit (Fig. 2a), then knit the next two stitches together. With the left needle, bring the slipped stitch over the stitch just made (Fig. 2b) and off the needle.

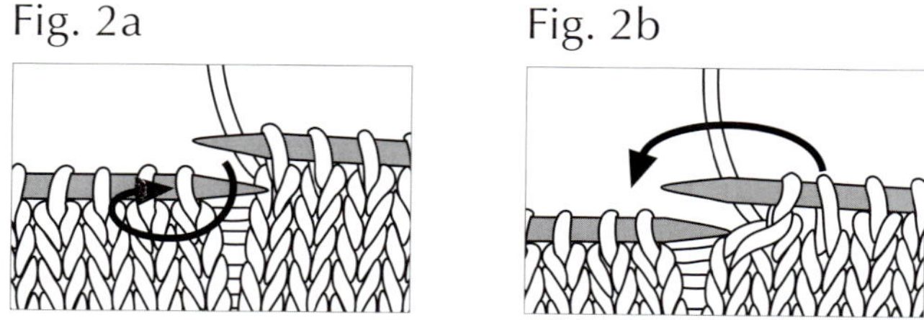

Fig. 2a

Fig. 2b

YARN OVER (abbreviated yo)

Bring the yarn forward between the needles, then back over the top of the right hand needle, so that it is now in position to knit the next stitch (Fig. 3).

Fig. 3

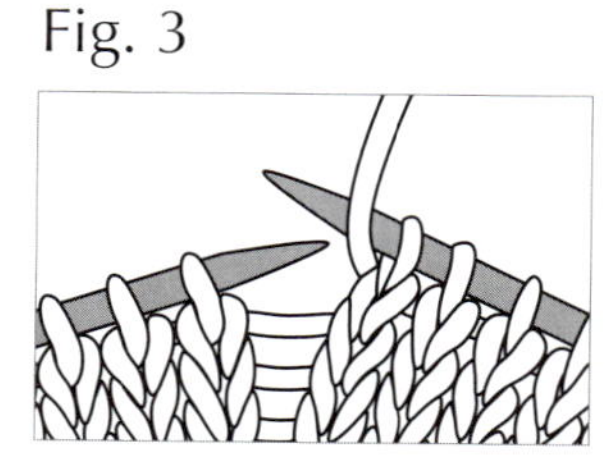

KNIT TERMINOLOGY	
UNITED STATES	**INTERNATIONAL**
gauge	= tension
bind off	= cast off
yarn over (YO)	= yarn forward (yfwd) **or**
	yarn around needle (yrn)

CROCHET TERMINOLOGY	
UNITED STATES	**INTERNATIONAL**
slip stitch (slip st)	= single crochet (sc)
single crochet (sc)	= double crochet (dc)
half double crochet (hdc)	= half treble crochet (htr)
double crochet (dc)	= treble crochet (tr)
treble crochet (tr)	= double treble crochet (dtr)
double treble crochet (dtr)	= triple treble crochet (ttr)
triple treble crochet (tr tr)	= quadruple treble crochet (qtr)
skip	= miss

Yarn Weight Symbol & Names	SUPER FINE 1	FINE 2	LIGHT 3	MEDIUM 4	BULKY 5	SUPER BULKY 6
Type of Yarns in Category	Sock, Fingering Baby	Sport, Baby	DK, Light Worsted	Worsted, Afghan, Aran	Chunky, Craft, Rug	Bulky, Roving
Knit Gauge Ranges in Stockinette St to 4" (10 cm)	27-32 sts	23-26 sts	21-24 sts	16-20 sts	12-15 sts	6-11 sts
Advised Needle Size Range	1-3	3-5	5-7	7-9	9-11	11 and larger
Crochet Gauge Ranges in Single Crochet to 4" (10 cm)	21-32 sts	16-20 sts	12-17 sts	11-14 sts	8-11 sts	5-9 sts
Advised Hook Size Range	B-1 to E-4	E-4 to 7	7 to I-9	I-9 to K-10.5	K-10.5 to M-13	M-13 and larger

KNITTING NEEDLES		
UNITED STATES	**ENGLISH U.K.**	**METRIC (mm)**
0	13	2
1	12	2.25
2	11	2.75
3	10	3.25
4	9	3.5
5	8	3.75
6	7	4
7	6	4.5
8	5	5
9	4	5.5
10	3	6
10½	2	6.5
11	1	8
13	00	9
15	000	10
17	---	12.75

CROCHET HOOKS	
UNITED STATES	**METRIC (mm)**
B-1	2.25
C-2	2.75
D-3	3.25
E-4	3.5
F-5	3.75
G-6	4
H-8	5
I-9	5.5
J-10	6
K-10½	6.5
N	9
P	10
Q	15

We have made every effort to ensure that these instructions are accurate and complete. We cannot, however, be responsible for human error, typographical mistakes, or variations in individual work.